Ha! Ha! Ha! Ha! Ha!

THE
FRIGHT
ZONE

Jokes, Riddles, Tongue Twisters & "Daffynitions"

By Gary Chmielewski

Illustrated by Jim Caputo

Read Jokes. Write Jokes.

Ha! Ha! Ha! Ha! Ha! Ha! Ha!

NORWOOD HOUSE PRESS

A Note to Parents and Caregivers:

As the old saying goes, "Laughter is the best medicine." It's true for reading as well. Kids naturally love humor, so why not look to their interests to get them motivated to read? The Funny Zone series features books that include jokes, riddles, word plays, and tongue twisters—all of which are sure to delight your young reader.

We invite you to share this book with your child, taking turns to read aloud to one another, practicing timing, emphasis, and expression. You and your child can deliver the jokes in a natural voice, or have fun creating character voices and exaggerating funny words. Be sure to pause often to make sure your child understands the jokes. Talk about what you are reading and use this opportunity to explore new vocabulary words and ideas. Reading aloud can help your child build confidence in reading.

Along with being fun and motivating, humorous text involves higher order thinking skills that support comprehension. Jokes, riddles, and word plays require us to explore the creative use of language, develop word and sound recognition, and expand vocabulary.

At the end of the book there are activities to help your child develop writing skills. These activities tap your child's creativity by exploring numerous types of humor. Children who write materials based on the activities are encouraged to send them to Norwood House Press for publication on our website or in future books. Please see page 24 for details.

Above all, the most important part of the reading experience is to have fun and enjoy it!

Sincerely,

Shannon Cannon

Shannon Cannon
Literacy Consultant

NorwoodHouse Press

P.O. Box 316598 • Chicago, Illinois 60631
For information regarding Norwood House Press, please visit our website at: www.norwoodhousepress.com or call 866-565-2900.

Editor: Jessy McCulloch
Designer: Design Lab

Library of Congress Cataloging-in-Publication Data:
Chmielewski, Gary, 1946–
  The fright zone / By Gary Chmielewski ; Illustrated by Jim Caputo.
     p. cm. — (The funny zone)
  Summary: "Book contains 100 monster-themed jokes, tongue twisters and "Daffynitions". Backmatter includes creative writing information and exercises. After completing the exercises, the reader is encouraged to write their own jokes and submit them for web site posting and future Funny Zone editions. Full-color illustrations throughout"—Provided by publisher.
  ISBN-13: 978-1-59953-298-1 (library edition : alk. paper)
  ISBN-10: 1-59953-298-0 (library edition : alk. paper) 1.
Supernatural—Juvenile humor. 2. Monsters—Juvenile humor. I. Caputo, Jim. II. Title.
  PN6231.S877C46 2009
  809'.9337—dc22   2008033634

Manufactured in the United States of America in North Mankato, Minnesota 163R-052010

PAR FOR THE CORPSE

Why didn't the zombie go to school?
He was feeling rotten!

What's the scariest thing about flying Zombie Airlines?
The fright attendants!

Do zombies like being dead?
Of corpse (*course*)!

What kind of streets do zombies like the best?
Dead-end streets!

What theory do giggling zombies prove?
That there is laugh after death!

How would you describe the expression on a zombie's face?
Deadpan!

What is one thing you can't sell to a zombie?
Life insurance!

HERE A WOLF, THERE A WOLF...

What's a werewolf's favorite day of the week?
Moon-day!

What do you call a hairy beast that is lost?
A *where-wolf!*

Why do werewolves do so well in school?
They give snappy answers!

Where do you store a werewolf?
In a *were-house!*

What do you call a horrible dream in which a werewolf is attacking you?
A *bite-mare!*

NOW YOU SEE HIM...

Why did the invisible man go insane?
Out of sight, out of mind!

Why did the girl stop dating the invisible man?
She wasn't able to see enough of him!

Doctor to the invisible man:
"This is a difficult diagnosis. Nothing seems to show up on any of your tests."

Why did the invisible man look in the mirror?
To see if he still wasn't there!

Why did the invisible mother take her child to the doctor?
To find out why he wasn't all there!

The nurse walked into the busy doctor's office and said, "Doctor, the invisible man is here."
The doctor replied: "Sorry, I can't see him now."

SPELLBOUND

What type of music do witches play on the piano?
Hag-time!

How do you make a witch itch?
Take away her "w"!

Which story do little witches like to hear at bedtime?
"Ghoul Deluxe and the Three Scares"!

What does a witch ask for when she goes to a hotel?
Broom service!

Why won't a witch wear a flat cap?
There's no point to it!

Why did the witch consult an astrologer?
She wanted to know her **horror**-scope!

What do you get if you cross a witch and an iceberg?
A cold spell!

Why do witches get good bargains?
They like to **haggle**!

What kind of tests do they give in witch school?
Hex-aminations!

TODAY'S LESSON:
SPELLS AND HEXES

CLAP
CLAP
CLAP

Why is a witch like a candle?
Both are wicked!

Why do witches only ride their brooms after dark?
That's the time to go to sweep!

What happened to the naughty little witch at school?
She was ex-spelled!

Why did the witches go on strike?
They wanted sweeping reforms.

What would you find on a haunted beach?
A *sandwitch*

Why do witches think they're funny?
Every time they look in the mirror, it cracks up!

What is the witches' motto?
"We came, we saw, we conjured!"

What happens if you see twin witches?
You won't know which witch is which!

Which is the witch that wishes the wicked wish?

What happened to the little witches who ate all of their vegetables?
They *grewsome!*

Why did the witch put her broom in the wash?
She wanted a clean sweep!

Have you heard about the good weather witch?
She forecasts sunny spells!

Why couldn't the young witch find a job?
She didn't have enough hex-perience!

What do you call two witches living together?
Broom-mates!

What do you call a witch's garage?
A broom closet!

Why do witches go around scaring people?
They're just trying to eek out a living!

What do witches wear to bed?
Fright-gowns!

What color hair do most witches have?
Brewnette!

How do witches play their records?
In scarey-o!

What does a witch serve her friends?
A four-curse meal!

What do witches read to their babies to help them sleep?
Scary tales and dreadtime stories!

How many witches does it take to change a light bulb?
Just one, but she changes it into a toad!

Why did the warlock get lost in the woods?
He didn't know *witch* way to go!

THE BONE ZONE

How did the skeleton know it was raining?
He could feel it in his bones!

Why didn't the skeleton go to the party?
He had no body to go with!

Why didn't the skeleton like his job?
His heart wasn't in it!

What do you say to a skeleton crew when it goes sailing?
"*Bone* voyage!"

What's a skeleton's favorite musical instrument?
Trom-bone!

What kind of plates do skeletons eat off of?
Bone china!

Why are skeletons usually so calm?
Nothing gets under their skin!

What do you call a skeleton who won't get up in the morning?
A lazy bones!

Why did the skeleton go dancing?
To see the boogie man!

Why do skeletons hate winter?
The cold goes right through them!

13

THE GRAVEYARD SHIFT

What did one casket say to the other casket?
"Is that you *coffin?*"

What should you do to keep a corpse from smelling?
Nothing – dead people can't smell!

If you lived in a cemetery, what would you use to open the gate?
A skeleton key!

What runs around a cemetery but doesn't move?
A fence!

What was written on the hypochondriac's tombstone?
"I told you I was ill."

Why are cemeteries in the middle of town?
They're dead centers!

Why did the mortician have such a big party?
The morgue the merrier!

How do undertakers prepare for funerals?
They re-**hearse**!

Why did the gravedigger keep a pail on the sidewalk?
So someone would kick the bucket!

Why were there long lines at the cemetery?
People were dying to get in!

How do you know that you are talking to an undertaker?
By his *grave* manner!

BLOOD RELATIONS

Why does Dracula consider himself a good artist?
He likes to draw blood!

What do you give a vampire with a cold?
Coffin drops!

How many vampires does it take to change a light bulb?
None! Vampires like the dark.

What's Dracula's favorite flavor of ice cream?
Vein-illa!

How does a vampire girl flirt?
She *bats* her eyes!

What do you think of Dracula's films?
Fang-tastic!

What's Dracula's favorite coffee?
Decoffinated!

Why is Hollywood full of vampires?
They always need someone to play the *bit* parts!

What did the vampire call his new false teeth?
A new fangled device!

What time do vampires hate?
Daylight Savings Time!

What do false teeth and vampires have in common?
The both come out at night!

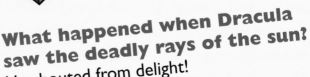

What happened when Dracula saw the deadly rays of the sun?
He shouted from delight!

Why did the vampire get sick after lunch?
He ate a *stake* sandwich!

What's a vampire's favorite holiday?
Fangsgiving!

What's a vampire's favorite animal?
A giraffe!

Did you hear the one about the vampire?
It was a *vein* attempt at humor!

What song does Dracula hate?
"You Are My Sunshine"!

What's it like to be kissed by a vampire?
It's a pain in the neck!

What type of dogs do vampires like best?
Bloodhounds!

Why did the vampire's girlfriend dump him?
The relationship was too draining!

Where does Count Dracula usually eat his lunch?
At the casketeria!

Why did the vampire run screaming out of the restaurant?
He found out it was a *stake* house!

What do they feed vampires for their last meal?
Stake and potatoes!

Why did the other kids have to let the vampire play baseball?
It was his *bat*!

What's a vampire's favorite sport?

Batminton!

What's a vampire's favorite soap opera?

"The Guiding Bite"

Do you think Dracula can get the job done?

Sure, he's very cape-able!

How do vampires like their food served?

In bite-sized pieces!

What do you get when you cross a snowman with a vampire?
Frostbite!

What's a vampire's favorite game?
"Follow the Bleeder"

Why doesn't Dracula do well on a blind date?
All the girls think that he's a little batty!

Patient: "Can you treat me for a vampire bite?"
Doctor: "Neck's weak?"
Patient: "No, next week will be too late!"

How do you stop the pain of vampire bites?
Don't bite any!

Why was Count Dracula glad to help young vampires?
He liked to see new blood in the business!

MUMMY DEAREST

Did you see the play about the mummies?
Too bad, it wrapped already!

Why do mummies make excellent spies?
They're good at keeping things under wraps!

Where do mummies go for a swim?
In the Dead Sea!

Why was the mummy so tense and grouchy?
He was all wound up!

Why don't mummies take vacations?
They're afraid they'll relax and unwind!

What is a mummy's favorite type of music?
Wrap!

Why do mummies have trouble keeping friends?
They're too wrapped up in themselves!

News Bulletin …
Mummies are not evil!
They just get a bad wrap!

Why couldn't the mummy answer the phone?
He was all tied up!

What do you call a mummies convention?
A *wrap* session!

Why are Egyptian children so good?
They respect their mummies!

Why was the mummy sent into the game as a pinch-hitter?
With a mummy at bat, the game would be all wrapped up!

Where do mummies go when they visit Arizona?
The Petrified Forest!

How can you tell when a mummy is angry?
He flips his lid!

WRITING JOKES CAN BE AS MUCH FUN AS READING THEM!

A pun is a joke that uses words in funny ways. One way to make a pun is to take a word that sounds a lot like another word (or words). Next you switch the words, or make a play on words, to create the joke. It is important to remember that puns are very short and you get to the punch line quickly. You can often take a pun and turn it into a riddle. Here is an example from page 14:

What did one casket say to the other casket?

"Is that you coffin?"

This is funny because *coffin* is another word for casket, and it sounds a lot like the word *coughing*.

Go back and re-read the jokes in this book. Which of them are puns? Which ones do you think are funny? Try to figure out why you think they are funny.

YOU TRY IT!

Here is a joke-writing exercise you can do by yourself or with some friends who enjoy things that are scary. Find a book of scary stories. You could even use this joke book. Pick out some words that refer to scary things. Try to think of words or short phrases that sound very similar to the words you picked. Then come up with jokes that use the plays on words you've come up with. Now practice the jokes on some people. Just make sure that they know a little about your scary subjects, because if they don't, they won't understand your jokes! Keep the jokes that get big laughs, and keep working on the ones that don't.

SEND US YOUR JOKES!

Pick out the best puns that you created and send them to us at Norwood House Press. We will publish it on our website — organized according to grade level, the state you live in, and your first name.

Selected jokes might also appear in a future special edition book, *Kids Write in the Funny Zone*. If your joke is included in the book, you and your school will receive a free copy.

Here's how to send the jokes to Norwood House Press:

1) Go to www.norwoodhousepress.com.
2) Click on the **Enter the Funny Zone** tab.
3) Select and print the joke submission form.
4) Fill out the form, include your joke, and send to:
   The Funny Zone
   Norwood House Press
   PO Box 316598
   Chicago, IL 60631

Here's how to see your joke posted on the website:

1) Go to www.norwoodhousepress.com.
2) Click on the **Enter the Funny Zone** tab.
3) Select **Kids Write in the Funny Zone** tab.
4) Locate your grade level, then state, then first name.
   If it's not there yet check back again.